Dwight Whitney Marsh

Manual of the Congregational Church and Society in Owego

Dwight Whitney Marsh

Manual of the Congregational Church and Society in Owego

ISBN/EAN: 9783337043179

Printed in Europe, USA, Canada, Australia, Japan

Cover: Foto ©ninafisch / pixelio.de

More available books at **www.hansebooks.com**

OF THE

Congregational Church and Society

IN

OWEGO,

Tioga County, New York.

SEPTEMBER 1, 1874.

OWEGO:
BEEBE & KINGMAN, PRINTERS,
1874.

OF THE

Congregational Church and Society

IN

OWEGO,

Tioga County, New York.

SEPTEMBER 1, 1874.

OWEGO:
BEEBE & KINGMAN, PRINTERS,
No. 30 LAKE STREET.

1874.

Prepared by Order of the Church.

JONATHAN TENNEY,
FRANK L. JONES,
DWIGHT W. MARSH,
JOHN J. HOOKER,
JAMES M. HASTINGS,

Committee.

☞ Read EZEKIEL xliii: 11, 12.

ROMANS xii: 4, 5.

JOHN xvii: 11.

OFFICERS

OF THE

CHURCH and SOCIETY

For the Year 1874.

Annual Meeting and Election last Wednesday in December

DWIGHT W. MARSH,

Acting Pastor.

Deacons,
JOHN J. HOOKER,
JAMES M. HASTINGS,
JOHN B. G. BABCOCK.

FRANK L. JONES, Moderator.
DWIGHT W. MARSH, Clerk
CHAUNCEY HUNGERFORD, Treasurer.

Prudential Committee,
(WITH THE OTHER CHURCH OFFICERS,)
JONATHAN TENNEY.
DAVID GOODRICH,
DeFOREST MARSTERS.

Trustees of Society,

ANNUAL MEETING AND ELECTION, FIRST TUESDAY IN AUGUST.

LEE N. CHAMBERLAIN,	Term expires,	1874.
MILES F. HOWES,	" "	1874.
JERRY M. HOLLENSWORTH,	" "	1875.
JOHN J. HOOKER, Treasurer,	" "	1875.
BENJAMIN W. BROWN,	" "	1876.
JAMES M. HASTINGS, Clerk,	" "	1876.

Present Officers

OF

CHURCH AND SOCIETY.

Pastor.

DWIGHT W. MARSH.

Deacons.

JOHN J. HOOKER,　　JAMES M. HASTINGS,
JOHN B. G. BABCOCK.

FRANK L. JONES, MODERATOR.
DWIGHT W. MARSH, CLERK.
CHAUNCEY HUNGERFORD, TREASURER.

Prudential Committee.

ABOVE OFFICERS, AND

A. H. PHILLIPS,　　　JAMES HUTCHINSON,
DeFOREST MARSTERS.

Trustees of Society.

	Term Expires.
J. M. HOLLENSWORTH, - - - -	1875.
JOHN J. HOOKER, Treasurer, - - - -	1875.
BENJAMIN W. BROWN, - - - -	1876.
JAMES M. HASTINGS, Clerk, - - - -	1876.
L. N. CHAMBERLAIN, - - - - -	1877.
MICHAEL BERGIN, - - - - -	1877.

Music Committee for 1875.

DWIGHT W. MARSH,　R. B. HOWELL,　　M. BERGIN.

MANUAL.

Confession of Faith.

I. We believe that there is only one God, the Creator, Preserver and Moral Governor of the Universe; a Being of infinite power, knowledge, wisdom, justice, goodness and truth; the self-existent, independent and immutable fountain of good. Deut. 6: 4. Ex. 6: 3. Ex. 3: 14. Ps. 90: 2.. Isa. 45: 5. Jer. 10: 10. John 17: 3.

II. We believe that the scriptures of the Old and New Testament were given by inspiration of God; that they are profitable for doctrine, for correction, for reproof, and for instruction in righteousness, and that they are our only rule of doctrinal belief and religious practice. 2 Tim. 3: 17. 2 Peter 1: 19-21. Luke 24: 27. John 5: 39. Heb. 1: 1-2. Isa. 8: 20. Gal. 1: 8. 2 John 9: 11. Ps. 19:7—11.

III. We believe that the mode of divine existence is such as lays a foundation for three distinctions—the Father, the Son, and the Holy Ghost, and that these three are one in essence and equal in power and glory. Matt. 28: 19. 2 Cor. 13: 14. Rev. 14: 7. Ex. 34: 14, compared with Rev. 1: 5-6. Rev. 5: 8-13. Heb. 1: 6-8. Heb. 13: 8. John 1: 1-9. Phil. 2: 1-10. Acts 5: 3-4. Acts 13: 2-4.

IV. We believe that God has made all things for himself; that known unto him are all his works from the beginning; and that he governs all things according to the counsel of his own will. Ps. 19: 1. Rev. 4: 11. Isa. 45: 7. Acts 15: 18. Acts 2: 23. Isa. 46: 10. Eph. 1: 11.

V. We believe that the divine law and the principles and administration of the divine government are perfectly holy, just and good; and that all rational beings are bound to love and obey them. Isa. 45: 5. Jer. 10: 10. 1 Tim. 1: 17. Acts 14: 17. 1 Chron 29: 11-12. Deut. 4: 8. Psalm 119.

VI. We believe that God, at first, created man in his own image, in a state of rectitude and holiness, and that he fell from that state by transgressing the divine command. Gen. 1 : 26-27. Col. 3 : 10. Ecc. 7 : 29. Rom. 5 : 12.

VII. We believe that, in consequence of the apostasy, man, in his natural state, is destitute of holiness, and in opposition to the law, character, and government of God ; and that all men, previous to regeneration, are dead in trespasses and sins. Rom. 4 : 12. Rom 8 : 6-8. Eph. 2 : 3. Gen. 6 : 5. Ecc. 9 : 3. Ps. 14 : 1-3. Jer. 17 : 9. Rom. 8 : 6-8.

VIII. We believe that Christ the Son of God, has, by his obedience, sufferings, and death, made atonement for sin ; that he is the only Redeemer of sinners, and that all who are saved, will be altogether indebted to the grace and mercy of God, for their salvation. Heb. 2 : 14-16. John 1 : 14. 1 John 2 : 2. Rom. 5 : 8. Rev. 5 : 9. 1 Peter 1 : 18-20. Phil. 2 : 6-8. 1 Tim. 3 : 16. Matt. 26 : 28. Heb. 7 : 27.

IX. We believe that, although the invitations of the gospel are such, that whosoever will may come and take of the waters of life freely, yet the depravity of human nature is such, that no man will come to Christ, except the Father, by the special and efficacious influence of his spirit, draw him. Rev. 22 : 17. Isa. 45 : 22. Ezk. 18 : 30-31. Ezk. 33 : 11. Mark 16 : 15-16. John 5 : 40. Luke 14 : 7. Tit. 3 : 5. John 3 : 3.

X. We believe that those who embrace the gospel, were chosen of Christ from before the foundation of the world, that they should be holy and without blame before him in love ; and that they are saved not by works of righteousness which they have done, but according to the distinguishing mercy of God, through sanctification of the Spirit, and belief of the truth. Eph. 1 : 3-5. 2 Thess. 2 : 13. Rom. 9 : 18-21. Acts 13 : 48. Rev. 7 : 9-10. John 10 : 11-27. John 17 : 24. Rom. 8 : 29.

XI. We believe that those who cordially embrace Christ, although they may be left to fall into sin, never will be left finally to fall away and perish ; but will be kept by the power of God, through faith, unto repentance and salvation. Phil. 1 : 6. 1 Peter 1 : 3-5. Job 17 : 9. Jude 24. John 10 : 27-28. Rom. 8 : 38-39.

XII. We believe that watchfulness over the life; careful meditation: a conscientious attendance upon public, family, and secret worship; the steady practice of righteousness, truth, sincerity and charity towards man ; and of sobriety, chastity and temperance towards ourselves, are the indispensable duties of every christian. John 15 : 14-8-12. Matt. 10 : 37. Luke 6 : 46. James 1 : 26-27. James 3 : 17. Ex. 20 : 8-11. Luke 13 ; 10. 4 : 16. Acts 13 : 42. 16 : 13. Gen. 18 : 19. Deut. 6 : 6-7. 1 Cor. 6 : 10.

XIII. We believe that there will be a resurrection of the spiritual bodies, both of the just and of the unjust. John 5 : 28–29. Acts 26 : 8. 24 : 15. 1 Cor. 15 : 52. Dan. 12 : 2. 1 Cor. 15. Luke 20 : 57–58.

XIV. We believe that all mankind must, one day, come before the judgment seat of Christ, and receive final sentence of retribution according to the deeds done in the body; and that, then, the state of all will be fixed; and that the punishment of the wicked, and the happiness of the righteous will be righteously determined. 2 Cor. 5 : 10. Acts 17 : 30-31. John 5 : 22–23. Rev. 20 : 12. Rom. 2 : 11–12–16. Jude 14 : 15. 2 Thess. 1 : 6-10. Matt. 25 : 31–46.

XV. We believe that Christ has a visible church in the world, into which none but real believers in the sight of God have a right to admission. Matt. 18 : 17. Acts 2 : 47. 8 : 3. Matt. 16 : 18.

XVI. We believe that the sacraments of the New Testament are Baptism and the Lord's Supper; that true believers in Him only have a right to partake of the Lord's Supper, and that visible believers only, with their households, should be admitted to the ordinance of baptism. Matt. 28 : 19. Luke 22 : 19-20. Acts 8 : 36. Gen. 17: 7, compared with Gal. 3 : 17, and 1 Cor. 1 : 16. Acts 16 : 15.

Thus do you believe?

☞ The ordinance of Baptism, if not previously received, will here be administered.

To Those Baptized in Childhood.

You received the ordinance of baptism in your childhood, having been presented therefor by Christian parents (or guardians) who, in your behalf, trusted in the mercy of God for you through Jesus Christ. Do you now thankfully and solemnly ratify their act, and accept it as your own?

Form of Covenant.

You do now, in the presence of God and man, avouch the Lord, Jehovah, Father, Son, and Holy Ghost, to be your God, the supreme object of your affection, and your chosen portion forever. You cordially acknowledge the Lord Jesus Christ in his mediatorial offices, Prophet, Priest and King, as your only Savior and final Judge; and the Holy Spirit as your Sanctifier, Comforter, and Guide. You humhly and cheerfully devote yourself to God, in the everlas'ing covenant of His grace.

You consecrate all your powers and faculties to His service and glory; and you promise to take the Scriptures as the rule of your life and conversation; and that, through the assistance of His spirit and grace, you will cleave to Him as your chief good; that you will give diligent attention to His word and ordinances, to family and secret prayer, and to the observance of the Sabbath; that you will seek the honor of His name, and the interests of His kingdom; and that, henceforth denying all ungodliness and every worldly lust, you will live soberly, righteously and godly in the world.

You do now cordially join yourself to this as a church of Chris', engaging to submit to its discipline, so far as conformable to the rules of the Gospel; and, solemnly covenanting to strive, as much as in you lies, for its peace, edification and purity—to walk with its members in Christian love, faithfulness, circumspection, meekness, temperance, and sobriety; and, abandoning the sinful pleasures and amusements of the world—to prove what is that good and acceptable and perfect will of God.

Do you thus covenant and promise?

———

Form for the Admission of Members From Other Churches,

[Here those who unite by letter will rise in their places]

BELOVED FRIENDS.—In presenting yourselves for union with this Church, you in effect, renew your vows as the disciples of the Savior.

You accept the Confession of Faith adopted by this Church, and declare your hearty belief in the substance of the doctrines which it contains.

You, also, cordially join yourselves to this Church, and engage to submit to its rules and discipline; to labor for its purity, peace, and edification; with the grace of God assisting you, to be to it examples of the Spirit of Christ, and to walk with its members in faithfulness and wisdom, in meekness, temperance, sobriety and love.

This you promise?

The church arises.

We, the members of this Church, most affectionately receive you to our communion. We welcome you to this fellowship with us, in the enjoyment of the Gospel, and in labors for its spread. And we promise to watch over you, in love and fidelity ; to surround you with our sympathies ; to remember you in our prayers ; to commune with you of our Savior, and to seek continually your meetness for Heaven. And may the Lord Jehovah, Savior and Comforter, through the blood of the everlasting covenant, make you perfect in every good work, to do His will, working in you and us that which is well-pleasing in His sight, through Jesus Christ ; to whom be glory, for ever.   AMEN.

Covenant at the Baptism of Children.

[Parents are requested to present, in writing, to the Minister, the full name of each child]

You, who now present your children, to receive upon them the seal of God's covenant, profess yourselves believers in God and his Son, our Savior, and in the truth and the continuance of His promise to His children, to be a Father to them and to their seed after them. You covenant, on your part, in the presence of God, and of these witnesses, to train these children, whom He hath given you, in the nurture and admonition of the Lord ; to instruct them in the knowl- edge of all Divine Truth, as you may have opportunity, but especially in the Way of Salvation through Jesus Christ ; to walk before them daily, as God may give you grace, in the beauty of a cheerful and holy Christian life ; to seek, as your chief aim concerning them, their renewal of heart, and their salvation in the Redeemer ; and to labor, in all ways, with devout and prayerful endeavor, to prepare them to accomplish God's will on Earth, and to enter His rest and glory in Heaven.

Do you thus promise ?

Questions for Self-Examination.

The following Questions are affectionately recommended to the prayerful and frequent perusal of each member of this Church :

1. Are you in the practice of daily secret prayer ?

2. Are you in the practice of daily family prayer ?

3. Do you daily, with a prayerful desire to improve in Christian knowledge, read the Word of God ?

4. Do you make it a matter of conscience to attend all the meetings for social worship appointed by the Church, except as the providence of God shall otherwise direct ?

5. Is your *property* consecrated to Christ ?

6. Do you cultivate a spirit of Christian tenderness towards your brethren ?

7. Do you labor to keep your heart constantly alive to a sense of obligation, I. To God ; II. To all the friends of the Saviour; and, III. To your perishing fellow-creatures ?

Ecclesiastical Principles and Rules.

I. This Church claims the right of self-government, and holds itself amenable to no other ecclesiastical body, except by its own consent and in accordance with the established usages of Congregational Churches.

II. This Church is under obligations to extend to other evangelical Churches that fellowship called in the scriptures, "The Communion of Saints," and such advice and assistance as may be sought and recognized by a common discipleship to a common Savior ; and, in like manner, to receive the same from them.

III. An opportunity will be given, at such times as may be most convenient, for Christian parents to present their infant children for the ordinance of baptism. At such times, parents are expected to present in writing, their own names, together with the full name of each child, and the place and date of its birth, that the same may be entered by the clerk on the records of the Church. Children are admitted to baptism when either parent is a member of an Evangelical Christian Church.

IV. Application for church membership, by letter or profession, shall be presented at a regular church meeting, and after due examination and recommendation of the Prudential Committee, candidates may, if approved by vote of the Church, become members on giving public assent to the Articles of Faith and Covenant.

V. Members are expected, permanently on removing from this parish, to ask for letters of dismission and recommendation. Requests for such letters may be announced at any regular church meeting, and, if granted by the vote of the church, the clerk shall prepare and forward the proper certificate.

VI. When a member of a sister church statedly worships and communes with this Church for more than one year, without uniting with it, the clerk shall notify the said person and the church of which he is a member, of the propriety of his entering into full communion with this local church.

VII. This Church considers immoral conduct, breach of Covenant Vows, neglect of acknowledged religious or relative duties, and avowed disbelief of the Articles of Faith to which all members have assented. as offenses subject to the discipline of the Church.

VIII. Any complaint against offending members must first be presented to the Prudential Committee, who shall, upon sufficient cause, present the case to the Church. But no complaint shall be entertained by this committee unless the means of reconciliation, and of reclaiming the offender as indicated by Christ in the XVIII Chapter of Matthew, shall, if possible, have been duly employed. An accused member shall be seasonably furnished with a copy of the complaint, and shall have a opportunity for a full hearing before the committee and the Church.

IX. The censure that may be inflicted on offenders are private reproof, public admonition, suspension, or excommunication, according to the aggravation of the offense; and, in case of excommunication, notice thereof shall be announced from the pulpit on the Sabbath following.

X. The stated officers of the Church shall be Pastor or Pastors, Deacons, Moderator, Clerk, Treasurer and three other members of the Church, who, with the above mentioned officers, shall constitute a Prudential Committee.

XI. The Pastor shall be elected in accordance with the basis of Union hereinafter given, and be installed by advice and assistance of a Council. All other officers thus far named shall be chosen by ballot, without formal nomination ; and all elections determined by a majority of members of lawful age, present and voting. Vacancies in any of the offices occurring between the annual meetings, may be filled at any business meeting,—such meeting, with its object, having been notified from the pulpit, the previous Sabbath.

XII. The number of Deacons shall be, at least, three, who shall be elected for a term of three years,—one retiring each year, the rank being decided by lot at the first election. Before entering upon their duties, they may be set apart by prayer and the laying on of hands. It shall be the special duty of the Deacons to assist the Pastor in the spiritual care of the Church, in the administration of the Lord's Supper, in the distribution of the charities of the Church ; also in presiding at religious meetings for which no other provision is made ; and to provide for the pulpit in the absence, or at the request, of the Pastor.

XIII. The Clerk shall keep a record of the doings of the Church, of its standing regulations, and of its members, with the time of their admission, dismission, and death, so far as can be ascertained. He shall, also, record the names of children baptized, under the proper date, with the date of their birth and the names of their parents. At the annual meeting, he shall give a written report of the state of the Church, with its history during the previous year, and an account of members received and removed.

XIV. The Treasurer shall take charge of Church collections, and at the annual meeting, report in writing, by items, all Church moneys received and paid out by him.

XV. The duties of the Prudential Committee shall be to guard the spiritual welfare of the Church; conduct and report upon examinations for admission to the Church; and, dropping the Pastor, prepare and bring before the Church such cases for discipline as seem to require the notice of the Church.

XVI. Terms of Church officers, except that of Pastor, shall expire on the last day of December, annually, or until their successors are elected.

XVII. All business meetings shall be opened by prayer. The Pastor may act as Moderator, unless the Moderator chosen be present.

The regular meetings of the church shall be at the time of the stated preparatory lecture before each communion service, which shall be on the first Sabbath of each alternate month, beginning with the first Sabbath in February, 1874; also, at a corresponding time in each intervening month. Annual meetings for election of officers shall be on the last Wednesday evening in December, with the following order of business:—

1. Reading minutes of last annual meeting.
2. Annual reports of officers.
3. Proposed amendments to Ecclesiastical Principles and Rules.
4. Election of officers.
5. Miscellaneous business.

XVIII. The Confession of Faith, Covenant, Form of Admission, and Ecclesiastical Principles and Rules, may be altered only at an annual meeting, and by vote of two-thirds of the members of lawful age present and voting. Notice of such alteration, in a written form, must be given at some previous meeting of the church.

Rules for Business Meetings.

The decisions of the presiding officer are subject to revision by the Church.

Motions must be made in writing, *if required* by any member .

A motion, resolution or amendment may be withdrawn by the mover, before a vote upon it has been taken.

Privileged motions, which may be made at any time, are motions to postpone indefinitely, to refer to a committee, to lay on the table, to postpone to a future fixed time, and to adjourn,—all of which may be debated except the last named.

When a member is speaking, no motion can be made without his consent.

The proposition *last made* is always the one under consideration, and the first to be voted on.

If several *sums* are proposed, the *largest* is to be first put to vote; if several *times*, the *longest*.

The usual mode of voting is by the uplifted hand.

A member who has a motion to make, may preface it with remarks to explain his design ; but, with this exception, speaking is out of order, unless some definite proposition has been duly submitted and under consideration, after being seconded.

Basis of Union

BETWEEN THE CHURCH AND THE SOCIETY.

1.   The Society shall hold the property, and receive the income, and make all pecuniary engagements, appropriations, and payments.

2.   In calling a Pastor, the Society and Church shall act as concurrent bodies,—a majority of each being necessary to constitute a call; the Church first nominating, and the Society confirming or rejecting the nomination.

The Church will provide for the supply of the pulpit when there is no settled Pastor ; make the necessary arrangements for singing, and, in general, for the orderly observance of religious worship ; and the Society will liquidate all reasonable expenses thereby incurred.

Digest of the Laws of the State of New York

IN RELATION TO ECCLESIASTICAL ORGANIZATIONS.

ELECTION OF TRUSTEES AT THE ORIGINAL FORMATION OF A SOCIETY.

1. Public notice must be given, where the congregation statedly worships, at least fifteen days before the said organization and election, and on two successive Sabbaths.

2. Two members of the congregation, to be nominated by a majority of the members present, shall preside at the election, receive the ballots of the electors, and be the judges of the qualifications of such elections ; and after the election, they shall certify, under their hands and seals, the names of the persons elected as Trustees, the corporate name adopted, and have the same acknowledged and recorded in the County Clerk's Office.

3. Only male persons of lawful age are entitled to vote.

4. No person who has not statedly worshiped with the congregation, or been considered a member, can vote.

5. Not less than three, nor more than nine, persons shall be elected as Trustees.

6. A plurality of votes shall decide the election.

SEAL OF THE TRUSTEES.

The Trustees shall have and use a common Seal, which may be altered or renewed at pleasure.

POWER OF THE TRUSTEES.

1. They shall take and hold possession of all the property of the Society, both real and personal.

2. In their corporate name they can sue and be sued.

3. They have power to repair and alter their places of worship, and, if necessary, to erect a new edifice, and also to purchase or build a dwelling house for the Pastor.

4. They may make rules for managing the temporal affairs of the Society.

5. May dispose of the income of the Society according to their judgment.

6. Shall regulate the prices, and order the renting of pews.

7. Shall appoint a Clerk and Treasurer of the Board, who may be removed at pleasure.

MEETINGS OF TRUSTEES.

Any two of the Trustees shall have power to call a special meeting of the Board.

A majority of the whole number of Trustees only shall have power to attend to business at any meeting lawfully convened.

TRUSTEES TO BE DIVIDED INTO CLASSES.

The Trustees first chosen at the organization of any religious Society, shall be divided into three classes, to the intent that one-third of the members of the Board shall vacate their office at the end of each year.

After the first election, all Trustees shall hold their office for the term of three years.

NOTICE OF NEW ELECTIONS OF TRUSTEES.

The Trustees, or a majority of them, shall, at least one month before the expiration of the office of any of the Trustees, notify the same in writing to the Minister, or in case of his death or absence, to the Deacons, specifying the names of those whose term will expire; and the said Minister or Deacons shall give fifteen days' notice to the congregation, on two successive Sabbaths, of a new election, which election shall be held at least six days before such vacancies shall occur.

Any two members present, appointed by the Society, may preside at the election.

DEATH OF TRUSTEES, REMOVAL, ETC.

All vacancies by death, removal, or refusal to act, shall be filled in the same manner, and with the same public notice given, as at the regular elections.

VOTERS, AFTER THE ORIGINAL FORMATION OF ANY RELIGIOUS SOCIETY.

No person belonging to the Society shall be entitled to vote at any election succeeding the first, until he shall have been a stated attendant on Divine Worship at least *one year* before such election, and shall have contributed to the support of said Society, according to the useges and customs thereof.

The Clerk of the Board of Trustees shall keep a register of the names of the legal voters, and shall at all elections decide upon their qualifications.

MINISTER'S SALARY.

The Trustees shall not have power to fix upon the sum to be paid the Minister for his support, but the same shall be determined by a majority of legal voters, at a meeting to be called for that purpose.

REDUCING THE NUMBER OF TRUSTEES.

The Society may reduce the number of their Trustees at any annual meeting, provided said number be not less than three.

ANNUAL MEETING.

It shall be lawful for any Society, at its stated annual meeting, to alter and fix the time for the next annual meeting and election of Trustees.

Congregational Principles.

I. DEFINITION OF A CHURCH.—A Christian Church is a voluntary association of professed believers in Christ, united by solemn covenant for the public worship of God, for the enjoyment of Christian ordinances, and for mutual aid in christian duties.

II. OF THE NAME, CONGREGATIONAL.—The term Congregational is applied to our Churches, because all ecclesiastical power resides, not in the officers, but in *the congregated body*, or *members* of the Church. The Congregational plan corresponds, in all its essential features, with that of the Apostolic or New Testament Churches, and, by its freedom, tends greatly to promote *individual* activity and growth.

III. OFFICERS.—The Officers of a Congregational Church, in spiritual things, are of two orders only,—Pastors and Deacons. In the New Testament, Pastors are styled Bishops, Presbyters, or Elders, the words being synonymous. It is usual, however, to appoint occasional and standing committees, to co-operate with the Pastor and Deacons in performing such duties as the Church may assign to them.

IV. RIGHTS AND POWERS OF THE CHURCH.—Each local Church is complete in itself, and possesses all the powers and privileges incident to a Church of Christ, e. g. :

1. The power of choosing and removing its own officers.
2. "   "   forming its own creed.
3. "   "   admitting and excluding members.
4. "   "   regulating the details of its own Worship and modes of procedure.

Other powers might be specified, but it is sufficient to state that all the affairs of a Congregational Church are determined by a vote of the adult members, and, in some cases, by the brethren only.

V. RIGHTS AND DUTIES OF MEMBERS.—The Members of a Congregational Church are on an *equality* as to privilege and obligation. They are all alike responsible for the well-being of the body, so that *personal exertion* on the part of each member, becomes a constant and pressing duty. Every member is therefore expected and considered as voluntarily bound, to be diligent in private and social duties; to attend habitually the stated meetings of the Church, especially on the Sabbath; and to do all in his or her power to exemplify the doctrines of the Gospel, and to spread it through the world.

VI. FORM OF CHURCH ORGANIZATION AND INTERCOURSE WITH OTHER CHURCHES.—It would seem, *from the nature of the case*, that the first Churches must have been Congregational. The earliest admission of members to a Christian Church, after Christ's ascension, was that in

Jerusalem, of which we read the account in Acts, 2d chapter. To what body could this first Church have been responsible? With what connected? How could it have stood, except as an independent Church, complete in itself—a truly Congregational Church?

It appears also, *from Scripture and from History*, that the early Churches were Congregational.

Other Churches besides that at Jerusalem are spoken of as equally complete, and are designated by the names of the several places where they were formed, as The Church at Antioch, The Church at Corinth, the Church at Ephesus.

The Sacred Writers do not even represent the Christians of a single Province as embraced in one Church ; for they speak of "the *Churches* of Macedonia," "the *Churches* of Asia,"—not of *the Church* of Macedonia or Asia. Hence, we infer that every company of believers who covenant together for Church purposes is a complete Church of Christ. Each separate Church, also, is represented as exercising, itself, the appropriate functions of a Church of Christ, for

1. Business of importance was intrusted *by the whole Church* to its messengers, Acts xv: 2, 3; these messengers were received by *the body of the Church*, xv: 4; answer was returned from the *whole company of the brethren*, xv: 22, 3, and was carried to the *whole* "multitude" of the Church, xv: 30.

2. Officers were elected by the body of disciples, viz: An Apostle Acts I: 15, 22—26, and Deacons, VI: 5.

3. Discipline was administered by the body of disciples. See 1 Cor. v: 4, where the Church, as a body, are supposed to be "gathered together;" 2 Cor. II: 6, 7, where the discipline is spoken of as " the punishment inflicted of many," implying, evidently, the agency of the *body of the Church in it ;* Matt. XVIII: 17, where the Savior directs those who have been offended, as their last resort, to " tell it *to the Church.*

The testimony of ancient history coincides with the above views: Mosheim remarks that " with regard to government and internal economy, *every individual Church considered itself an independent community,* none of them ever looking, in these respects, beyond the circle of its own members, or recognizing any sort of external influence or authority."—Mosheim, v. 1, 196.

Gibbon says, "the societies which were instituted in the cities of the Roman Empire were united only by the ties of faith and charity. Independence and Equality formed the basis of their internal constitution."—Decline and Fall, vol. 1, 554.

Dr. Owen affirms "that in no approved writers for the space of two hundred years after Christ, is there any mention made of any other organical visibly professing Church but that only which is parochial or congregational."—Punchard, 158.

While, then, Congregationalists admit the duty of deference to Pastors and teachers in the Church, as their spiritual guides in the doctrine of Christ, they believe the whole Church is responsible, through its individual members, for the maintenance of doctrinal pu rity, and of discipline, and that this responsibility cannot be delega- ted by them to others, nor be taken from them without departing from the simple and spiritual institutions of the Gospel.

Though preferring, on Scriptural grounds and grounds of expedi- ency, the organization and principles of their own Churches, Con- gregationalists recognise all societies of believers who lov e our Lord Jesus Christ in truth and sincerity. They invite to their Commun- ion members in good standing in other Churches, and practise the usual interchange of members by letters of dismission and recom- mendation.

VII. ECCLESIASTICAL BODIES.—Those generally recognized by Con- gregational Churches are Councils, Conferences, Consociations, As- sociations, and General Associations.

Councils are advisory bodies, meeting by invitation, and composed of Pastors and delegates from Churches.

Conferences are assemblies of neighboring Churches for spiritual advancement.

Consociations are stated meetings of ministers and lay delegates for advancement of the interests of the Churches and for personal edification.

Associations are usually gatherings of Ministers only for profes- si onal improvement.

The General Association is composed of delegates from the smaller Associations. It meets annually; hearers reports on the state of relig- ion; suggests advice to the Churches as to the concerns of benevo- lence, sound doctrine, and religious duty.

It will be particularly noted that all these bodies are simply advis- ory. None of them possess any *ecclesiastical power;* and the Church- es may, if they choose, manage their concerns without them. Still, so much confidence is reposed in the character, wisdom and piety of these bodies, that great weight is cheerfully given to their opinion.

Thus the independence of Congregational Churches is neither Dis- cord nor Isolation. On the contrary, they live in close fraternal union; ask and receive advice and assistance from each other ; and may admonish each other in case of heresy, lax discipline, or any scandalous offense. But it is *fellowship* that is recognized, not *de- pendence of one upon another* for existence or for rights.

Historical and Statistical.

In preparing this part of the MANUAL, great diligence has been exercised, at the expense of much correspondence, examination of records and other papers, and personal inquiry, to make it accurate and complete. But no claim is made that this object has been fully attained. Of the nearly 25 years since the existence of the Church, records of only about 12 can be found; and of these there is, for the most part, evidence of great inaccuracy. This remark is made, not only as due to the compiler, but as a kind suggestion to the future clerks of the Church. Of the organization of the Church, and the history of its earlier life during the ministry of Rev. Mr. Wilcox, not a line can be found on record. Some of the most important events in the subsequent movements of the Church, respecting revivals, settlements and dismissals of ministers, baptisms, admissions, discipline, &c., &c., are entirely omittted, or mentioned in a very unsatisfactory manner. The first Manual was printed in 1857, and contained the names of the membership at that date, arranged alphabetically. The next appeared in 1867. Both are full of errors, many of which are here corrected; but not a few, probably, still exist. A desire to approximate perfection has delayed the issue of the MANUAL beyond the first intention; and lack of room within the prescribed limits to print other interesting facts, especially of the early members, has compelled omission of much matter collected.

It is now impossible to know how many members were admitted at the organization of the Church, or during the ministries of Rev. Messrs. Wilcox, Kidder, Corning, Bartlett, Gould, Tyler, and Page. Those of the four later ministers are nearly, if not quite, correct.

For facts under this head, special obligation is due to Rev. D. D. Gregory's Tioga Presbytery, Messrs. Beebe & Kingman, for files of the Owego *Gazette;* F. E. Platt, Esq., for access to records of the Presbyterian sessions; Hon. A. H. Calhoun, Col. B. B. Curry, Gordon Bliss, Mrs. Mary C. Wilcox, Mrs. Mary S. Walker, and many others.

Corrections or additions will be gratefully received by either of the Committee named on the 2d page.

Congregationalism in Owego.

It is said that Owego, in its early history, "long bore the character of an irreligious place." Yet, before the close of the last century, there were many godly people settled here. They came mostly from New England, and brought with them the religious faith and church polity of the Pilgrims of Plymouth. Immediately following them came ministers of like faith and polity—men of deep piety and missionary zeal, mostly from Connecticut, and graduates of Yale and

Dartmouth. They preached and founded churches wherever they could find opportunity. Osborne, Loring, Chapin, Weed and Williston were leading lights among these early missionaries; and, as says Rev. Mr. Gregory, "the churches they formed were of the Congregational order."

"But," says the same writer, "until about the year 1833, there was no rivalry or sectarian jealousy between Presbyterians and Congregationalists. They preached, and prayed, and won souls, and built Christ's church, with remarkable brotherly kindness." Each church, composed of members of both Congregational and Presbyterian antecedents and preferences, was advised by the "Plan of Union" formed, in 1801, to join presbytery or association, as convenience of location or other circumstances might determine to be expedient, while adopting such church polity as the majority preferred.

The anti-slavery controversy ruptured the Presbyterian Church in 1837, carried away the "Plan of Union" of 36 years, and many churches, once presbyterian in name, withdrew and united themselves with "associations" similar to those they knew in New England. Sharper distinctions were consequently made in church polity.

Prior to this, as long ago as 1803, at Lisle, Broome county, on the occasion of the ordination of Rev. Seth Williston, was formed the "Susquehanna Congregational Association," the first clerical organization in Southern Central New York.

Among the results of the labors of Levi Hart, of Yale, Seth Williston, of Dartmouth, and others, was the organization of the "Owego Congregational Society," August 7, 1810. Under this name it continued 43 years, or until June 4, 1853, more than three years after the formation of the "*Independent* Congregational Society of Owego." Its name was then changed, by legislative enactment, to the "First Presbyterian Society in the Village of Owego."

In connection with this society of 1810, a church was formed, July 24, 1817, by Revs. Hezekiah May, Jeremiah Osborne, and William Wisner, called "The Owego Congregational Church." In July, 1831, it partially adopted the Presbyterian Church polity, and elected four ruling elders. It appears, however, that, for some years after, the membership was allowed to hear and decide upon cases of doctrine and discipline after the Congregational mode. The "close sessions," however, were always displeasing to many in the church, who were still firmly attached to the freedom of action and open discipline of its earlier history. Between 1831 and 1849, vigorous efforts were frequently made to effect a return to pure Congregationalism. Failing of success in these efforts, several members resolved to take steps toward forming a new church of the Congregational order.

From the records of the Presbyterian Church of Owego, it appears that, on Monday, Dec. 31, 1849, "the session" held a special meeting, at which were present Rev. Philip C. Hay, Moderator ; William Platt, William Pumpelly, Francis Armstrong, Joseph A. Beecher, Jared Huntington, Marcus LaMonte, Lambert Beecher, Elders. The following 46 persons were, at their own request, dismissed, for the purpose of forming a Congregational Church, viz.: Andrew H. Calhoun, James W. Lamoureux, Newell Matson, Flora M. Matson, Abner T. True, Lydia True, Erastus Meacham, Betsey Meacham, Erastus Dodge, Mercie Dodge, James Hutchinson, Minerva A. Hutchinson, Penoni F. Curry, Maria C. Curry, Gilbert Williams, Anne E. Wiliams, Laforest B. Cooley, Caroline E. Cooley, Noah Goodrich, Charlotte L. Goodrich, Beriah H. Truesdell, Catharine B. Truesdell, John Perry, Mary Perry, John A. Lefler, Lucia E. Lefler, John Frank, Sally Frank, Joseph Dodge, Charity Dodge, Erastus Goodrich, Hope Goodrich, Gordon Bliss, Lura Bliss, Henry W. Camp, Phebe H. Truesdell, Mary M. Hollister, Starr B. Smith, Charlotte Dodge, Jane Dodge, Sarah J. Williams, Minerva Beebe, Huldah Munson, Jerusha Ketchum, Jane True, Jane Kimball True."

The Owego *Gazette*, of Feb. 21, 1850, has the following local item : " The Congregationalists organized into a distinct church on Tuesday last (Feb. 19, 1850). Rev. Richard Salter Storrs, of Brooklyn, preached an appropriate discourse in the afternoon, and Rev. Joseph P. Thompson, of New York, in the evening. The charge to the new Church, by Rev. Dr. Storrs, was very affecting, and the entire service was, in the highest degree, interesting."

The Ecclesiastical Council that assisted in the organization of this church held its session in the Presbyterian lecture room, at 9 A. M., in accordance with public notice, two weeks previous. The services of the afternoon and evening were held in the Presbyterian church. Andrew H. Calhoun, Newell Matson, James W. Lamoureux, Abner T. True, and Henry W. Camp, were the Committee of Arrangements. The following is a copy of the paper presented to the Council by this Committee:

To the Ecclesiastical Council convened at Owego, February 19, 1850, *for the purpose of organizing a Congregational Church:*

In organizing as a church of Christ, and in asking the aid of a Council to assist in that organization, we are influenced only by a sense of duty and a desire to place ourselves under that form of church government which we deem most in accordance with Scripture rules. A very considerable number of us were brought up Congregationalists, and we still sacredly regard our early associations, and cling with fervor and affection to that form of church government which our fathers adopted, and under which their churches have prospered. Some of us became members of the Presbyterian Church from necessity rather than choice—there being no Congregational church here at the time of our connection ; and subscribing fully to the articles of faith and covenant, as adopted by that church in its original Congregational organization, we did not deem the difference in government a sufficient reason to debar ourselves from the privileges and duties of membership. Some of us were members when the church was Congregational ; and notwithstanding the supposed necessity which seemed to require it to adopt the Presbyterian form of government, we have ever retained a preference for this mode in which we were nurtured.

In separating from that church, we desire not to place ourselves in an antagonistic position. We love that church. Its great object is, also, our object; and our long association has endeared us to its members. We object, only, to its mode of government, and in this dissent we are earnest and conscientious. We like not a government vested in a bench of Elders, because they are more likely to be swayed by extraneous influences than the whole body ; nor can they be supposed to represent the wishes of the church. They act as the church without consultation with its members, or a knowledge of their desires ; and it may happen that they as frequently carry out the design of the minister, who, from his position, often wields a potent influence, as of the church they profess to represent ; and sometimes cases will arise in which the church and the minister are at issue. In a word, the minister and elders *are the church*, while the great body of members are mere *ciphers.*

The effect of this system is felt in all the ramifications of church business. The occasional meeting of the elders, or session, who constitute, in reality, *the church*, seems to preclude the necessity of calling together the whole body, because, in business matters, the members have no part nor lot. Hence, it is not unfrequent—nay, it is a fact to which all can testify—that members of the same church are often not even personally acquainted with each other. They are not present at the examination of candidates for membership, and see them only when that act is consummated. They know nothing of the Christian character of those whom they are publicly called upon to fellowship, other than the fact that they have passed the ordeal required by the rules of the church, and they *must* be satisfied. In our view, this tends to lessen spirituality among the members, and coldness, apathy and worldliness assumes its place

We prefer a Congregational form of government, because all the members of the church, as such, are under equal obligations and are entitled to equal privileges. They receive or dismiss, judge upon hearing the accused, and thus become acquainted with, and interested in, the welfare of each one of their brethren. The responsibility of administering its offices vests equally upon all who associated, and hence each individual feels the more sensibly, and understands the more fully, the duties and importance of his station. In this view we are fully borne out by Scripture rule. Christ says : "Moreover, if thy brother shall trespass against thee, go and tell him his fault between him and thee alone ; if he shall hear thee, thou hast gained thy brother. But if he will not hear thee, then take with thee one or two more, that in the mouth of two or three witnesses every word may be established. And if he shall neglect to hear them, tell it unto the church ; but if he neglect to hear the church, let him be unto thee as a heathen man and a publican."

We are of the opinion that the term *church*, as here spoken of, means the whole body of its members—not a delegated few ; and if Christ intended that the voice of the church be requisite to *expel*, then, by parity of reasoning, the church, as a church, possesses fully the governing power. But it is not our design to institute a comparison between Presbyterianism and Congregationalism. It is sufficient for our purpose to say, that we prefer the Congregational mode of government, and desire to return to it. The country around is rapidly filling up, and many of those settling in our midst emigrate from a Congregational community. These want a home, and we are desirous to provide one for them ; and in doing so we wish not to infringe upon, or interfere with, the rights of other denominations.

To conclude, we depart from our Presbyterian brethren in sorrow, not in anger. We have been long associated with them, and we love the doctrines and cherish the sentiments of the articles of faith under which we have been united. A difference of opinion in regard to government shall not lead us to disparage their sincerity as Christians, nor their usefulness in promoting the interest of Christ's kingdom. We love them as co-workers in the cause of God, and we will stand by and aid in all their efforts to extend the precepts and influences of our holy religion. Thus, though differing in what is not essential to salvation, yet conscientiously believing our views to be those of the Bible, we will harmonize and act with them in the great work of man's redemption, praying that the only strife which shall ever exist between us shall be—which shall love God most and serve Him best.

With this brief exposition of our views and feelings, we respectfully ask an organization under the Congregational mode of government, to be called the Owego *Congregational Church.*

In behalf of the applicants,

ANDREW H. CALHOUN.
NEWELL MATSON.
HENRY W. CAMP.
JAMES W. LAMOUREUX.

OWEGO, Feb. 19, 1850.

For a copy of this valuable paper, the compiler is indebted to its author, Hon. A. H. Calhoun, late of Brooklyn, N. Y., and, also, for the interesting letter which accompanied the same, extracts from which seem pertinent to this sketch :

NEW YORK, Jan. 22, 1874.

DEAR SIR,—I have your note of the 17th inst., asking for any information I may be able to give in relation to the organization of the Congregational Society of Owego. As an active participant in that "notable event," and a life-time admirer of Congregationalism, I comply with your request with great pleasure, and shall rejoice if I can be of any service to you in the preparation of your proposed historical sketch. The lapse of a quarter of a century, however, *may* have somewhat impaired my memory, though from the great interest I took in the matter at the time, and the deep solicitude I have ever felt in the prosperity of the Owego church, I recall the circumstances of the organization as an event of yesterday.

The present Presbyterian church in Owego was founded as a *Congregational* church ; but in the course of years, without any official, or church, action on the subject, it slid into the Presbyterian form, and continued for many years to prosper as a Presbyterian church. Such was its condition when the project of a distinct Congregational church was started. At first, it was proposed to attempt a return to its original form of government ; but it soon became apparent that this could not be effected harmoniously, and the design was abandoned. The effort for a Congregational church was then urgently pressed ; and the existence of the present flourishing society attests the wisdom of the movement.

In the formation of a new church, there was nothing of a spirit of rivalry, or a desire to detract from the influence or usefulness of any other organization. On the contrary, it was felt that a co-laborer in the cause of Christ was needed, and that an additional helper would essentially aid the advancement of the Redeemer's kingdom. There was no feeling of envy, distrust or dissatisfaction with our Presbyterian brethren, from whom the most of us had parted ; no heart burnings ; no real or fancied wrongs to redress ; no desire to interfere with their purposes in any particular, but simply to establish a new gospel branch in accordance with our ideas of church government, with a view of co-operating with them in the same great work in which they had been so long and usefully engaged. We desired, too, a home for new comers of Congregational proclivities, judging that it would be more congenial with their views and feelings to worship in their own temple and be governed by their own rules. Animated with such feelings, the organization of the Congregational church was pressed, and, consequently, no obstruction impeded its progress. Within a short time the church was organized, and the event was consummated in entire harmony with the other Christian denominations. The two churches immediately interested exhibited toward each other the most brotherly Christian feelings and good will, and a general sentiment of " God speed and bless both churches," seemed to be manifest on every countenance.

The church was organized in the month of February, 1850, by Rev. Doct. Thompson, of the Tabernacle, New York, and Rev. Dr. Storrs, of the Pilgrim, Brooklyn, who were invited for that purpose. Rev. Mr. Wilcox, the first pastor of the church, and Rev. Dr. Hay, of the Presbyterian church, were also present. The services were very impressive, and were listened to by a large audience with great interest. A statement, giving the reasons for organizing a new church, was read by the undersigned. Entire harmony and good will prevailed.

Respectfully yours,

A. H. CALHOUN.

Prof. J. Tenney.

The Rev. Mr. Wilcox was immediately engaged as acting pastor, and services were statedly held in the Court House, corner of Main and Court streets, until the present church building was completed. The " Independent Congregational Society " was organized in the Court House, August 1, 1850. January 2, 1851, the Society bought of Hon. T. I. Chatfield, for $900, a lot on Park street for a church edifice. May 17, 1851, Chauncey Hungerford, under a contract for $5,100, commenced erecting a house of worship thereon.

This structure was ready for occupancy, and solemnly dedicated to the service of Almighty God, Feb. 3, 1852. Rev. R. E. Eggleston preached the sermon, and was assisted in the services by Rev. Messrs. Burlingame, Snyder, Wilcox, and Hay.

In accordance with a vote passed June 29, 1863, the conference room and church parlor were built, and alterations and repairs made, during the summer and autumn succeeding, at an expense of about $5000. An organ was also purchased and placed in the church.

During its existence of about 25 years, the church has employed 11 stated ministers, and been about two years without stated supply. Of these 11 only five have been installed as pastors, viz.: Rev. Messrs. Corning, Bartlett, Tyler, Everest, and Bulkley. These frequent changes have, no doubt, operated unfavorably upon the prosperity of the church. In spiritual as in other affairs, an overseer, not only talented, cultivated, devoted, wise, and popular, is needed, but also one who can lay foundations deep and strong, and build thereon structures high and massive. Time is needful for such work.

Sketches of the Ministers.

1. SAMUEL CORYLUS WILCOX was the real founder of this church, and his devoted labors for its welfare cost him his life. He was born in Sandisfield, Berkshire county, Mass., Dec. 21, 1809; graduated at Williams College in 1835; taught, the three following years, in Lenox Academy; graduated at Auburn Theological Seminary in 1840 ; supplied the Congregational pulpit in Berkshire, N. Y., one year ; began to supply the Presbyterian church in Owego in the latter part of 1841 ; was ordained and installed its pastor, May 24, 1842, as sucsessor of Rev. Dr. Charles White, late President of Wabash College ; resigned, April 30, 1846, on account of a lack of sympathy between himself and his elders on the subject of slavery and Congregational polity. In February, 1847, he went to Williamsburg, Mass., where he was, for two years, pastor of the Congregational church. In 1849, he returned to Owego, at the earnest solicitation of many of his former flock, who were anxious to form a new church and society. After this was accomplished by his aid and counsel, he was made acting pastor, and so remained until increasing ill health compelled him to resign his charge, September 11, 1853. He still resided here, and started a family and day school for boys about one and a half miles east of the village, which continued for some years under Rev. Mr. Kidder and others. His earthly labors closed March 26, 1854. It was a most glorious testimony to the power of the religion of Christ. "It is not hard to die; it is better than to live," said he, when told he was dying. When almost gone, he added, "Oh, it is not death; it is the beginning of life." He was frail in bodily strength; vigorous in intellect; brilliant as a pulpit orator, seldom using notes ; amiable in temper ; a pious and cheerful Christian, ever living in the full assurance of hope ; judicious and devoted as a pastor. Mr. W. was twice married ; (1) in 1840, to Almira Brewster, of Rochester, N. Y., who died in Owego, Sept. 1, 1843; (2) Dec. 1, 1846, to Mary S., daughter of Hon. William Darling, of Reading, Pa., and sister of Rev. Dr. Darling, of Albany, "an estimable lady, who cheered him in his work, and now survives him," residing in Philadelphia, Pa. "Remember how he spake unto you," are the words inscribed upon the marble slab that marks the place where sleeps his dust, in the old church-ground near the Presbyterian house of worship.

----

2. CORBIN KIDDER came to Owego as teacher and associate acting pastor with Rev. Mr. Wilcox, January, 1853 ; took entire charge of the church after Mr. W's resignation, Sept. 11, 1853, until Jan. 1, 1854, and continued to reside and teach in Owego until early in 1858, often supplying the pulpit in the absence of a pastor, and always an active member of the church. He was born in Wardsborough, Vt., June 1, 1801 ; graduated at Amherst College in 1828, and at Andover

Theological Seminary in 1832. July 30, 1834, he was ordained and settled pastor of the Congregational church in Saxonville, Mass.; left in 1857, and spent two years as agent of the American Tract Society. From 1839 to 1845, was pastor of the Congregational church in West Brattleborough, Vt. From thence, came to New York, and preached in Warsaw, Dryden, and Groton, between 1845 and 1853, when he came to Owego. From 1858 to 1862, he was pastor of the church in Spencer; from 1862 to 1866, in Churchville, Monroe county. In 1866, he went to Orland, Ind., and supplied the Missionary church there four years. After resting from labor for about two years, he began to preach in Poplar Grove, Ill., in 1873; but was lately laid aside from active duty by an attack of paralysis. He died Dec. 29, 1874. He has been a zealous and faithful worker for learning and religion during a long life. Dec. 2, 1840, he married Esther L. Wood, of Westminster, Mass., who died about 1870, leaving one son, Samuel Theodore Kidder now a divinity student at Yale. May 2, 1873, Mr. K. married Mrs. Marie Gorham, of Brooklyn, N. Y.

3. WILLIAM HENRY CORNING, the first settled pastor of this church, was born in Hartford, Conn., Dec. 15, 1820; graduated at Trinity College in 1842, and afterwards at Yale Theological Seminary. Was ordained and installed pastor of the Congregational church in Clinton, Mass., in 1848; left, by reason of ill health, in 1851. Began to preach in Owego, January, 1854; was installed pastor over this church, Mar. 8, 1854, and left May 1, 1857, after resignation and dismissal by council, with the reluctant consent of his people, March 31st, preceding. He was esteemed as a bold opponent of slavery and intemperance; deeply interested in not only the welfare of the church, but in schools and other matters of public interest; a pious and faithful pastor; a terse and vigorous writer and speaker, and a highly useful citizen. After a summer's rest, he took charge of the Presbyterian church in Whitehall, where he continued, struggling against disease and working as he could for his Master, until May, 1862. After this, he continued to fail in health, until he surrendered his earthly being at Saratoga Springs, Oct. 9, 1862. He was buried in his native city. Says a friend: "It was his meat and drink to preach the gospel. His unfinished sermons—the pen so reluctantly laid aside—tell of purposes broken off, of a sun gone down while it was yet day." Several of his sermons were published. March 3, 1854, he married Mary, daughter of Dr. Samuel Spring, of East Hartford, Conn., a niece of the late Rev. Dr. Gardiner Spring, of New York, a lady of talent and culture, who has written much, and well, in the interests of morality and religion. She now resides in Hartford, Conn., wife of Rev. J. B. R. Walker.

4. WILLIAM ALVIN BARTLETT preached here from Sept. 12, 1857, to Aug. 1, 1858. During this time he joined the church, Feb. 25th; was

ordained pastor in March; and dismissed, by council, at his own request, June 28th. He was eminently popular as a preacher, drawing crowded houses of delighted listeners to his gifted efforts. Sept. 5, 1858, he commenced his labors as pastor of the Elm Place Congregational church,. Brooklyn. N. Y., to which he had been invited the spring previous, and so continued until he was called to the pastorate of the Plymouth Congregational church in Chicago, Nov. 30, 1868, as successor to the beloved Rev Lewis E. Matson, whose new birth and early Christian nurture were under the sainted Wilcox and Corning in this church. Mr. B. was settled in Chicago, Feb. 14, 1869, and still remains there. He was born in Binghamton, Dec. 4, 1832 ; graduated at Hamilton College in 1852 ; studied theology at Union Theological Seminary ; went to Europe and studied at Berlin and at Halle, at the university of which he matriculated in 1857. He has written and published several sermons, a volume on ·· Military Heroes of the Bible," and other books, and contributed largely to the religious journals, especially the *Independent* and the *Advance*, of which latter paper he is one of the editors. March 17, 1859, he married Charlotte A. Flanders, lately deceased.

----

5. SAMUEL McLELLAN GOULD was born in Gorham, Me., Jan. 24, 1809 ; entered Bowdoin College in 1829, but did not graduate; studied theology with Rev. Asa Mead, East Hartford, Ct., and Rev. Drs. Beeman and Kirk, in Troy, N. Y.; was licensed to preach by Berkshire (Mass.) Congregational Association, and preached in various places in Eastern New York. About 1837, he was settled over a Presbyterian church in Norristown, Pa., where he remained until 1851. Jan. 6, 1853, he became pastor of the 1st Congregational church, Biddeford, Me.; remained until March, 1857, when, through his efforts, was formed the Pavilion Congregational church in the same city, which he supplied until he began to preach in Owego as acting pastor, Sept. 11, 1858. His stay here was brief, he having tendered his resignation Dec. 8, 1858, to take effect April 1, 1859. Since this latter date, he has preached in Allentown and Emporium, Pa., and now resides in Philadelphia. He has never married.

----

6. MOSES COIT TYLER was born in Griswold, Conn., Aug. 2, 1835 ; graduated at Yale College, 1857 ; studied theology at Andover Theological Seminary, in 1858–'59 ; began to preach here, May 1, 1859 ; was ordained and installed pastor, August 24, 1859; married Jennie H. Gilbert, New Haven, Ct., Oct. 26, 1859; resigned his pastorate on account of ill health, June 24, 1860. Soon after, he began to preach to the Congregational church in Poughkeepsie, where he remained two years. Health again failing, he went abroad in 1863 ; remained four years, pursuing studies in literature and history, writing for American journals, and lecturing in Great Britain upon America. Returning in 1867, he became Professor of the English Language and

Literature in the University of Michigan, at Ann Arbor, which position he held six years. In January, 1873, he became the literary editor of the *Christian Union*, New York city, which position he still holds.

7. WILLIAM W. PAGE came here, as acting pastor, from the Presbyterian church in Deposit, where he had preached only about six months, Dec. 9, 1860. It is thought he came from Fairfax C. H., Va., to that place. He remained in Owego until about Dec. 1, 1861. After much pains-taking, the writer can learn no more concerning his history.

8. CHARLES HALL EVEREST was born in New Lebanon, Columbia county, Feb. 14, 1837; graduated at Williams College in 1859; studied theology at Union Theological Seminary 1859, '60, '61; was ordained in Plymouth church, Brooklyn, Dec. 30, 1861, and at once became pastor over this church, in which position he labored with great success and remarkable acceptance, three years, from Jan. 1, 1862, to Dec. 31, 1864. During this ministry the church prospered; 121 were added to its membership, and the church building was remodeled and enlarged. Jan. 1, 1865, he became pastor of the Church of the Puritans, Brooklyn, N. Y., where he still remains. He married, Feb. 11, 1862, Maria L. Wadhams, in Litchfield, Ct.

9. CHARLES H. A. BULKLEY was born in Charleston, S. C., Dec. 22, 1819; graduated at New York University in 1839, and at Union Theological Seminary in 1842. Was ordained and settled in New Brunswick, N. J., December, 1842; founded Congregational church, Janesville, Wis., in June, 1844, and labored with it two years; settled over Presbyterian church, Mt. Morris, in 1847, where he married Miss Anna W———, Sept. 8, 1847; remained four years; settled over Reformed church, Ithaca, in 1851, and remained two years; formed a church in West Winsted, Ct., in 1854, and remained six years; preached two years in Paterson, N. J.; went as chaplain in the Union army, in 1861, and remained 17 months; preached in Clinton a few months. He began to preach in Owego, May 4, 1867; was installed pastor in June following, and remained until May 1, 1871, entirely consecrated to his work, " with signs following." In January, 1868, he became pastor of the Congregational church in Malone, Franklin county, where he still remains. He has published a little volume, entitled " Baptism of Fire," and many occasional sermons.

10. JAMES CHAPLAIN BEECHER was born in Boston, Mass., Jan. 8, 1828; graduated at Dartmouth College in 1848; studied theology at Andover Theological Seminary in 1857; was ordained May 7, 1858; has been seaman's chaplain at Canton, China; chaplain of volunteers and Lieut. Col. of a colored regiment during the war of the Rebellion.

After the war was over, he preached in various places for brief periods; came to Owego, as acting pastor of this church, May 4, 1867, and remained until May, 1871. In the autumn of 1871, he became acting pastor of the Congregational church in Poughkeepsie, which position he has lately (December, 1874) resigned. Mr. B. married (1) Mrs. Anna E. (Goodwin) Morse, of Newburyport, Mass.; (2) Frances B. Johnson, of Guilford, Ct.

---

11. Dwight Whitney Marsh was born in Dalton, Berkshire county, Mass., Nov. 5, 1823; graduated at Williams College in 1842; studied theology at Andover Theological Seminary in 1842-3; taught in St. Louis, Mo., 1843-1847; continued his theological studies at Union Theological Seminary two years, and graduated there in 1849; was ordained, Oct. 2, 1849; sailed Dec. 7, 1849, from Boston for Mosul, Turkey, as Missionary of A. B. C. F. M.; returned and spent a few months in the United States, in 1852-3; married, Oct. 19, 1852, Julia White Peck, of New York city; went back to Mosul, where his wife died, Aug. 12, 1859. In 1860, he returned, finally, to this country; lectured in various places on missions and missionary life in Turkey, and preached some months in Hinsdale, Mass., and Godfrey, Ill. Aug. 21, 1862, he married Elizabeth L Barron, daughter of Rev. E. L. Clarke, of Richmond, Mass., and immediately took charge of the Rochester Young Ladies' Female Seminary, where he remained five years. During this time he preached for a year in the Western House of Refuge. After this, in 1867-8, he preached in Monticello, Ill., and in 1869-71, at Whitney's Point. He became acting pastor of this church, Aug. 1, 1871, and so remains.

Membership.

Explanations.—The *Nos.* in the FIRST COLUMN are given for convenience in reference. So far as known, full names are given in the SECOND COLUMN; when the family names of married ladies are known, they are given in parenthesis, and placed next those of their husbands when both are members of this church; when the family name is not known, the married ladies are denoted by *Mrs.* The prefix, *Miss*, is omitted. In the THIRD COLUMN, under *admission*, so far as can be ascertained, the *year* is given, with *p.* for by professsion, and *l.* for by letter. In the FOURTH COLUMN, under *removal*, *dis.* denotes regularly dismissed to other churches; *w.*, withdrew irregularly to other churches; *r.*, removed in mode unknown; *sus.*, suspended for breach of covenant, to be restored only on proper return and confession; or for having so long been absent that residence and history are unknown; *ex.*, expulsion or withdrawal of fellowship; *d.*, deceased, followed by date where known. Where this column is blank, present membership is implied. Residences and places of decease, otherwise than Owego, are given, so far as can be learned, in the FIFTH COLUMN.

No.	Name.	Admission.	Removal.	Residence and Remarks.
1	Abbott, Juliette (Williams) (Newton.)	p 1863	ex	Berkshire.
2	Agnew, Thomas H		d 1855	
3	Allen, Fanny Mrs		dis	Mother of Mrs. W. L. Hoskins.
4	Allen, Sylvester S		dis 1869	Newark Valley.
5	Allen, Nancy (Chapman.)		dis 1869	Newark Valley.
6	Allen, Clara M	p 1868	dis 1869	Newark Valley.
7	Andrus, Daniel S		dis	Williamsport, Pa.
8	Andrus, Adeline Mrs		dis	Williamsport, P.M.
9	Anneville, Charles	p 1863		
10	Anneville, Anna L. Mrs	p 1866		
11	Archibald, James	p 1863	sus 1873	
12	Archibald, Jennie	p 1871		
13	Babcock, John B. Gibson	p 1866		
14	Babcock, Lonisa Mrs	p 1866	d April 27, 1872	
15	Babcock, Emma J	p 1866		
16	Babcock, Zachary Taylor	p 1866		
17	Babcock, Alice (Chapman.)	1 1874		
18	Babcock, Sarah (Williams.)	p 1863	dis 1873	
19	Bacon, Mary R. (Clapp.)	1 1862		
20	Bacon, Mary Emma	p 1868	d April 19, 1871	
21	Bacon, Nellie Rebecca	p 1874		
22	Bacon, Charles Henry	p 1874		
23	Bailey, Henrietta (Doane)	p 1866	sus 1873	Gilboa.
24	Ball, Amelia (Hooker.)		dis 1870	Cleveland, O.
25	Barrett, Anna V. (Babcock.)	p 1866	d 1867	Cleveland, O.
26	Barrett, Charlotte D. (Babcock.)	p 1863	dis 1874	Cleveland, O.
27	Bartlett, William Alvin	1 1858	dis	
28	Barton, Helen C. Mrs	p 1871	dis	Chicago, Ill.

No.	Name		Year		Date	Year	Residence
29	Beebe, Adin	1	1850	d			Lisle Road.
30	Beebe, Minerva (Stone.)	1	1850	d			Lisle Road.
31	Benley, Augusta (Bostwick.)						
32	Bergen, Catherine (McBeth.)						
33	Berray, George			sns		1873	Walton.
34	Bignall, Juliette (Crater.)			d	January 15,	1862	Candor.
35	Blackman, Sabin M.	—	1850	dis			Candor.
36	Blackman, Mary L. Mrs			dis		1868	Hockanum, Conn.
37	Bliss, Gordon	1	1850	dis/d	June 3,	1868 / 1872	Hockanum, Conn.
38	Bliss, Luna (Phelps.)	p	1850	d			
39	Bloodgood, Darwin Henry	p	1863	d			
40	Bloodgood, Rhoda A. (Slosson.)	1	1862				
41	Bloodgood, Cyrus Ladd	1	1862				
42	Bloodgood, Sarah J. (Bean.)	1	1863				
43	Brister, Frederick W	—	1864	d	March 29,	1871	Elmira.
44	Brown, Benjamin W	p	1863	sns			
45	Brown, Lydia (Camp.)	p	1863	dis			
46	Brown, Fanny	1	1863	dis			
47	Bulkley, Charles H. A	1	1866	dis		1867	Malone.
48	Bulkley, Anna M. Mrs	1	1866	dis		1868	Malone.
49	Bulkley, Isabella W	1	1866	dis		1868	Malone.
50	Bulkley, Anna F	1	1866	dis		1868	Malone.
51	Bundy, Sarah Mrs	1	1862	d		1868	Elmira.
52	Burt, James Madison	1	1862	d	March 3,	1870	Newark Valley.
53	Burt, Martha A. (Bulkley.)	1					Newark Valley.
54	Butler, Stephen		1863	dis			Binghamton.
55	Butler, Abigail		1850	d			Binghamton.
56	Cady, William Dwight	p	1863	dis		1874	Brooklyn.
57	Cady, Mary E. (Goodrich.)	1	1850	d	Dec. 17,	1874	Brooklyn.
58	Calhoun, Andrew Hamilton	1					

No.	Name	Admission		Removal	Residence and Remarks
59	Cafferty, Martha	p 1863	sus		New York City.
60	Calkins, Albertine(Curtis).	p 1864	dis	1873	Chillicothe, Mo.
61	Camp, Henry W	1 1850	dis / d	January 11, 1874	1866
62	Camp, Lucy Mrs		dis	1866	
63	Camp, Elizabeth S		d	March 23, 1857	
64	Camp, Abby		d	1863	
65	Camp, Maria Mrs	p 1864			
66	Carpenter, Laura Ann	1850	d		
67	Case, Calista Mrs		dis		1850 Topeka, Kan.
68	Chadwick, John		dis	1872	
69	Chaffee, Philena Mrs	p 1869			
70	Chamberlain, Rometta S. Mrs	1 1868	dis		Providence, R. I.
71	Champlin, Martha A	p 1863	dis		Newark Valley.
72	Chapman, Edgar E	1 1864	dis	1873	Berkshire.
73	Chapman, Edward N	1 1869	dis	1866	
74	Chatfield, John R		w	1870	
75	Chatfield, Abbie E. (Smith.)		w	1867	
76	Christiance, Charles		sus	1873	
77	Clapp, Polly (Woodward.)	1 1862			
78	Clapp, James Henry				
79	Clapp, Mary A (Dana.)				
80	Clapp, Clarence Foster	p 1868	d		
81	Clapp, Lizzie Gertrude	p 1874	dis		
82	Clark, Timothy	p	ex	Sept. 16, 1862	Battle of Antietam.
83	Clark, Eliza B. Mrs	p	dis	1874	Southfield, Mass.
84	Clark, Ralph			1874	Southfield, Mass.
85	Clark, Elizabeth A	p 1871	dis		

No.	Name		Admitted		Dismissed	Residence
86	Clark, Pamelia Mrs.	p			1870	Easthampton, Mass.
87	Clark, Sarah M. (Webster.)		1863	dis		Kasson, Minn.
88	Coburn, Betsey C					
89	Cole, William H	p	1864	dis	1874	Kewanee, Ill.
90	Cole, Bessie R. (Watson.)	p	1864	dis	1874	Kewanee, Ill
91	Collins, Catharine					
92	Cook, William			ex	1855	
93	Cook, Mary					
94	Cooley, LaForest B	-	1850			
95	Cooley, Caroline E. Mrs	-	1850			
96	Cooley, Benjamin F			dis	1861	Newark Valley.
97	Cooley, Elvia H. Mrs			dis	1861	Newark Valley.
98	Cooper, Elizabeth B. Mrs			d	1873	
99	Cooper, Miss			d	1865	
100	Corbin, Romanda, Mrs	p	1863	sus	1873	Warren, Pa.
101	Corbin, Ella	p	1863	sus	1873	Cincinnati, Ohio.
102	Corey, Calista	p	1871	dis	1872	Poughkeepsie.
103	Corey, Catharine	p	1863	sus	1867	
104	Cornell, George	l	1862			
105	Cornell, Elizabeth (Whitney)	l	1854	d	October 9, 1862	Saratoga Springs.
106	Corning, William H	l	1854	dis	1854	Hartford, Conn.
107	Corning, Mary (Spring)	l		dis	1870	Penn Yan.
108	Cowles, Frank W	l	1868	dis	1870	Penn Yan.
109	Cowles, Sarah M. Mrs	l	1868	dis		
110	Crandall, H					
111	Crane, Sarah	l	1850	dis	1857	
112	Crater, William	l	1850			
113	Crater, Augusta					
114	Crater, Samuel	p	1866	d	1866	
115	Crater, Marinda Mrs					
116	Crater, Marinda	p	1874			
117	Crawford, Charles H	l	1869	dis	1869	Oswego.

No.	Name.	Admission.	Removal.	Residence and Remarks.
118	Crotsley, Jerusha		dis	1865 Hornbrook, Pa.
119	Crotsley, Flora	p 1863	dis	1865 Hornbrook, Pa.
120	Crotsley, Sarah		dis	1865 Hornbrook, Pa.
121	Curry, Benoni Benjamin........	l 1850	dis	1857 Pleasant Valley, N. J.
122	Curry, Maria (Clarke) (Reeves)...	l 1850	dis	
123	Curry, Emma A........	l 1850	dis	
124	Curtis, Cicero B........		dis	New Haven, Conn.
125	Curtis, Mary C. Mrs........			
126	Curtis, John J........	p 1863	dis	Elmira.
127	Daggett, Hattie C........		dis	1863 Lockport, Ill.
128	Dana, Foster	l 1868	d June,	1872
129	Dana, Hepzibath Mrs........	l 1868	d	
130	Dana, Lizzie R. Mrs........	l 1865	dis	
131	Danforth, John........		dis	
132	Danforth, Mary E. Mrs........		d	
133	Danforth, Arthur C........		d	
134	Daniels, Mary J. (Kimball) (True)...	l 1850	w	
135	Darling, Juliette B. Mrs........	l 1866	dis	1871 Ithaca.
136	Darling, Watson E........	l 1867	dis	1871 Ithaca.
137	Daved, Evalyn C........	p 1874	d	
138	Davidson, Moses W	l 1862		1874
139	Davidson, Elizabeth A. Mrs........	l 1862	dis	
140	Davis, William T........		dis	
141	Davis, Mary Mrs........		sus	
142	Davy, Loretto (Greeno)			1873
143	Decker, Susan H. (Stevens)........		sus	
144	Deming, John........		sus	
145	De Valliere, Lydia (Hill)........	p 1866		1873 Harrisburg, Pa.

No.	Name		Year		Date	Place
146	Dickinson, Cornelia J. (Bloodgood.)	p	1863	dis	1866	New York City.
147	Dodge, Erastus	l	1850	d		Illinois.
148	Dodge, Mercy Mrs	l	1850	dis		Illinois.
149	Dodge, Joseph	l	1850	d		
150	Dodge, Charity Mrs	l	1850	dis		
151	Dodge, Chandler	l	1850	dis		
152	Dodge, Jane Mrs	l	1850	dis		
153	Dodge, Alfred	p	1863			
154	Dodge, Mary (Truman)	p	1863	dis		
155	Doolittle, Marcus			dis	1862	Elmira.
156	Doolittle, Marcus Mrs			dis	1862	Elmira.
157	Doolittle, J. Henderson	p	1863			Susquehanna, Pa.
158	Doolittle, Ellen (True)					Susquehanna, Pa.
159	Drake, Sarah J. (Mittaugh)	l				
160	Dryer, Charles		1861	dis	1857	
161	Dugan, Orpha			dis	1874	Elmira.
162	Durland, Charles O			dis		
163	Ellis, Lydia J Mrs			dis	1872	Chicago, Ill.
164	Evans, Thomas Jr			d	1872 } 1874	Chicago, Ill.
165	Evans, Jane (Kilborn.)			dis	1872	Chicago, Ill. Milport, Pa.
166	Evans, Arthur	p	1866	dis		
167	Falls, Sarah J. (Hicks.)	p				
168	Ferguson, Anna M. Mrs	p	1874			
169	Ferris, Lemuel N	p				
170	Ferris, Lucy M. (Manley)	p	1863	d		Newark Valley.
171	Fivas, Ophelia J. (Branch)			dis		Chicago, Ill.
172	Forman, Edward				Feb. 13, 1864	Killed, Erie Railway.
173	Forsyth, George	p	1863	dis		
174	Foster, William C					
175	Foster, Emma Mrs	p	1872	dis		
176	Fowle, William					

No.	Name.	Admission.		Removal.	Residence and Remarks.
177	Fowle, Eliza A. Mrs.				
178	Fowle, Emma.				
179	Fowle, Caroline.				
180	Frank, John	1	1850	dis	
181	Frank, Sally (Price)	1	1850	dis	
182	Fredenburg, Sarada.				
183	Garland, Mary	p	1864	d	1864
184	Garrison, Ann	p	1863	dis	1867
185	Gaskill, Joseph	p	1863	sus	1873
186	Gaskill, Jane Mrs.	p	1863	dis	1865
187	Gilson, Lucinda W. (Davidson)	p	1863	dis	1865
188	Gladden, Washington	p		d	1873 Tioga.
189	Gladden, Jennie O. (Cahoon)	p		dis	1857 Brooklyn.
190	Goodrich, Noah			dis	Brooklyn.
191	Goodrich, Charlotte (Lane)	1	1850		Tioga.
192	Goodrich, Erastus	1	1850	d	1854 Buffalo.
193	Goodrich, Hope Mrs.	1	1850	{ dls / d	Feb. 13, 1857 / 1865
194	Goodrich, David	p			
195	Goodrich, Fanny (Truman)	p	1872		
196	Goodrich, George Leland	p	1872		Tioga.
197	Goodrich, Harriet F. Mrs.	p	1872		Tioga.
198	Goodrich, Mary A. Mrs.	p	1872		Tioga.
199	Goodrich, Lyman Truman	p	1856		
200	Goodrich, Cynthia M. (Cornell)	p	1869		
201	Gorman, Emma (Fulcher)	1			
202	Gorman, Emma M.	p	1872		
203	Gray, Dorothy H. Mrs.	1	1867	dis	1873 LeRaysville, Pa.

No.	Name		Year	Status	Date	Year	Place
204	Gray, Cyrus Winthrop	l	1867	dis / d	October 21,	1873 / 1874	LeRaysville, Pa.
205	Gray, Lillie	p	1868	dis		1873	LeRaysville, Pa.
206	Gray, Maria E (Campbell.)	p	1863	dis		1874	Binghamton.
207	Greeno, Phebe Mrs			sus		1873	
208	Handy, Mary Mrs			sus		1873	
209	Hartley, John	p	1862	dis		1864	
210	Hartley, John Mrs	p	1862	dis		1864	
211	Hastings, Rebecca Mrs	p	1863				
212	Hastings, James Monroe	p	1863				
213	Hastings, Persis G. (Jenks.)	p	1870				
214	Havens, Rachel Mrs			d			Weathersfield, Conn.
215	Head, John	p	1870	ex		1855	
216	Head, Melinda (Meacham.)						
217	Higley, Emerson H	p		dis		1863	Chicago, Ill.
218	Higley, Henry M	l	1861	dis		1873	Friendship.
219	Higley, Annette (Brister.)			dis		1873	Friendship.
220	Higley, Julia						
221	Hill, Harriet E. (Madan.)			w		1866	
222	Hill, Mary J. (Walker.)						
223	Hoagland, Christiana						
224	Hodge, Henry J	p	1868	d		1863	
225	Hodge, Caroline A. (Madan.)				July,		
226	Hodge, Ella Antoinette			d			
227	Holder, Elizabeth E. (Muzzy.)						
228	Hollensworth, M. Amelia (Johnson.)	p	1874				
229	Holley, Morris N	l	1873				
230	Holley, Adelaide S. (Todd.)	l	1873				
231	Hollister, Mary M. (Havens.)	l	1850				
232	Holmes, Loren V						
233	Holmes, Sarah P. Mrs						
234	Holmes, D			dis			Ithaca.

No.	Name.	Admission.			Removal.	Residence and Remarks.
235	Holmes, D. Mrs.	l	1869	dis		
236	Hooker, Lucy B. Mrs.	p	1853	d	October,	1855 Ithaca. 1872
237	Hooker, John J.	p				
238	Hooker, Lucy E. Mrs.					
239	Hooker, Archie Sumner	p	1872			
240	Horton, Clinton	p	1866	sus		1873
241	Hosford, Elihu			dis		
242	Hosford, Elmira J. Mrs.			dis		
243	Hoskins, Watson L.	p	1858	w		
244	Hoskins, Frances (Allen.)	l		di-		1854
245	Hoskins, Candace Mrs.	l	1861	d	May 2,	1867 Connection'.
246	Hoskins, Julia M. Mrs.	p	1874			
247	Hoskins, Jennie M.	p	1872			
248	Houk, Sarah Mrs.		1864			
249	Houk, Lewis C.	p	1863			
250	Houk, Jane E. Mrs.	p	1874			
251	Houk, Martha J. Mrs.	l	1874			
252	Howell, Roger Bacon.	l	1872			
253	Howell, Therr a R. (Cooper.)	p	1874			
254	Howes, Joshua Ferris					
255	Howes, Charlotte Mrs.	p	1863			
256	Howes, Teresa E. Mrs.					
257	Howes, Rebecca Mrs.	p	1874			
258	Howes, Lulu Florence.	l	1864	dis		
259	Hulse, Emily					
260	Humphrey, Jane					1866 Deposit.
261	Hungerford, Chauncey	p	1852			
262	Hungerford, Arminda S. Mrs.	?	1863			

No.	Name		Year	Status	Date	Year	Place
263	Hungerford, Mortimer	p	1872				
264	Hungerford, Martha (Tierney) (Searles.)	p	1864	dis		1873	Ithaca.
265	Hunt, J. W. Mrs	l					
266	Hunt, Zoda B						
267	Hutchinson, James	l	1850				
268	Hutchinson, Minerva A. (Wilson.)	l	1850				
269	Hutchinson, Alice M	p	1863				
270	Hutchinson, Frank Jay	p	1872				
271	Hutchinson, Lilla A	p	1866				
272	Hyde, Otis Bennett	p	1864				
273	Hyde, Mary J. (Fulcher.)						
274	Hyde, Anna (Fulcher.)						
275	Hyde, Nellie W	p	1874				
276	Ireland, Thomas			dis			
277	Ireland, Caroline Mrs			dis			
278	Ireland, Evalina E			dis			
279	Ireland, William D			dis			
280	Ireland, Henrietta A	l	1866	dis		1868	Ithaca.
281	James, LeRoy A	p	1868	dis		1868	Ithaca.
282	James, Sarah A. (Slater.)	p	1866	d	June 4,	1868	Ithaca.
283	Johnson, James Henry	l	1869				
284	Johnson, Marion C. (Fritcher.)						
285	Johnson, Caroline (Ketchum)						
286	Johnson, Lelia	p	1866	w		1873	
287	Jones, Catharine						
288	Jones, Elizabeth Mrs	p	1864				
289	Jones, James Edward	p	1863	sus	March 18,	1873	
290	Jones, Amelia D. Mrs			d		1869	
291	Jones, Frank L	p	1866				
292	Jones, Hannah (Curtis.)	l	1873				
293	Jones, Ann	l	1866	d		1869	
294	Jones, George	l					

No.	Name	Admission		Removal	Residence and Remarks.
295	Joslyn, Rhoda				
296	Joslyn, Peter		r		
297	Joslyn, Sarah Mrs		r		
298	Keeler, Albert Harrison		sus	1873	
299	Keeler, Sarah (Hill.)	p	sus	1873	
300	Keeler, Charles H.	p	1863 dis	1867	
301	Keeler, Charles H. Mrs	l	1863 dis	1867	
302	Kent, Chauncey, Mrs		d		
303	Ketchum, Jerusha Mrs	l	1850		
304	Ketchum, Hamilton	p	1863 d	February, 1864	
305	Kidder, Corbin	l	dis		Poplar Grove, Ill.
306	Kidder, Esther L. (Wood.)	l	dis		Orland, Ind.
307	Kilbourn, George L	p	1866		Brooklyn
308	Kilbourn, Jennie M. Mrs	p	1866		Brooklyn.
309	Kingsley, John Flavel	p	1870		
310	Kingsley, Hannah A. (Barton.)	l	1870		
311	Kipp, Emma A. Mrs	p	1864		
312	Knapp, Maria				
313	Knapp, Mercy H.				
314	Lamonrenz, James Willard	l	1850 d	April 20, 1859	Southfield, Mo.
315	Lamonrenz, Phebe A. Mrs		dis	1865	Pa.
316	Lauders, Betsey Mrs				
317	Lane, Elizabeth		d	May 19, 1866	
318	Lane, Elizabeth W. Mrs	p	1863 {d / d}	1869 / 1874	} Williamsport, Pa.
319	Ledyard, Anna Viola	p	1863 sus	February, 1873	Union.
320	Lefler, John A.	l	1850 dis		Jersey City, N. J.
321	Lefler, Lucia E. Mrs	l	1850 dis		Jersey City, N. J.

No.	Name						
322	Lewis, Ellen Mrs.	p	1863	ex		1867	
323	Livermore, Cyrus E.	l	1873				
324	Livermore, Susan A. (Prentice)	l	1873				
325	Loring, Nellie C. Mrs.	l	1873				
326	Lown, Ellen	p	1864	dis		1873	
327	Mackley, Frank S.	p	1863	sus		1873	
328	Mackley, Sarah C.	p	1864	dis		1866	Syracuse.
329	Madan, Frances L.	p	1863				Hornellsville.
330	Malone, Adelia		1863	ex		1864	New York City.
331	Manning, Robert					1855	
332	Manning, Martha	s	1863	dis			
333	Manwaring, J. M.	l					
334	Marsh, Sarah (Whitney)	l	1873				
335	Marsh, Dwight Whitney	l	1873				
336	Marsh, Elizabeth L. (Clarke)	l	1873				
337	Marsters, DeForest	p	1871				
338	Marsters, Lucetta (Cass.)	p	1850				
339	Matson, Newell	l	1850	dis		1863	Chicago, Ill.
340	Matson, Flora M (Case.)	l		dis		1863	Chicago, Ill.
341	Matson, Lewis Emmons	p		dis d d	June 21, April 27,	1863 1868	Lyons, France.
342	Matson, Cynthia Mrs.			dis		1859	
343	Matson, Flora P.			d	July,	1863	
344	Mattison, William T.			dis		1872	Elmira.
345	Mattison, W. T. Mrs.			dis		1867	
346	Mayor, Mary (Camp.)			dis		1866	
347	McGuffey, Archibald	l	1853	dis			
348	McGuffey, Ellen	l	1853	dis			Buffalo.
349	McGuffey, Mary	l	1853	dis			Buffalo.
350	Meacham, Erastus	l	1850				
351	Meacham, Betsey (Lake)	l	1850				
352	Meacham, Myron E			sus		1873	Hornellsville.

No.	Name.	Admission.		Removal.		Residence and Remarks.
353	Meacham, Abby Mrs.		sus		1873	Hornellsville.
354	Measor, John E.	p 1862	dis		1867	Fairmount, Minn.
355	Measor, Louisa A. (Curry.)		dis		1867	Fairmount, Minn.
			d	Dec. 2,	1874	
356	Merrill, Miss	p 1863	sus		1873	
357	Mersereau, Carrie (Cafferty.)	p 1863	sus		1873	
358	Morehouse, Mary A. (Hill.)					
359	Morton, DeEtte	p 1863				
360	Munson, Huldah	p 1850				
361	Muzzy, Edward		sus		1873	
362	Muzzy, Julia A. (Sheldon.)		d	November,	1871,	
363	Muzzy, Mary E		sus		1867	
364	Muzzy, William					
365	Muzzy, William Mrs.		sus		1873	
366	Narsh, Ruby Ann	p 1866				
367	Newcomb, Sarah (Lawrence) (Clarke.)	l 1873				
368	Newell, Ella E. (Smith.)	p 1866	w			
369	Newell, Mary (Cooley.)	p 1863				
370	Nichols, George Mrs.	p 1863				
371	North, James Eli	l 1871				
372	North, Elmira E. (Smith.)	l 1871	w			
373	Ogden, Walter					
374	Ogden, Ethelbert	p 1863	dis			
375	Ogden, Elizabeth (Jones)					
376	Owen, Almira Mrs.				1868	
377	Owen, Thomas Mrs.					
378	Parmenter, Frederick A.	p 1863	dis			Elizabeth, N. J.
379	Parmenter, Elihu		d			Killed, Ithaca Railroad.

#	Name		Year	Status	Date	Year	Place
380	Perry, John	l	1850	d	January 20,	1853	
381	Perry, Mary (True)	l	1850	d	Nov. 20,	1856	
382	Peters, John	p	1866	sus		1873	
383	Peters, Mary Mrs	p	1863	sus		1873	
384	Phillips, Augustus H	p	1872				
385	Phillips, Ella C	p	1872				
386	Phillips, Mary A	p	1872				Mass.
387	Pierce, Mr	p	1863	dis			Mass.
388	Pierce, Mrs	p	1863	dis			
389	Porter, Caroline (Cole)	p	1863	dis		1867	
390	Prince, R	p	1863				
391	Probasco, Helen J. (Lown)	p	1864	dis		1873	Apalachin.
392	Purington, M. J. Mrs	p		dis		1866	Syracuse.
393	Purple, Elizabeth J. (Cooley)	p					Auburn.
394	Quimby, Ann Mrs	p	1869	d	Sept. 19,	1871	
395	Quimby, Martha						
396	Quimby, Sophia						
397	Raymond, Ellen (Comstock)	p	1863	dis		1867	
398	Reed, John A			sus		1873	Ithaca.
399	Reed, John A. Mrs			sus		1873	Ithaca.
400	Reeves, Edward P			ex		1857	
401	Reeves, Tapping						Ukiah, Cal.
402	Reeves, Lucinda						
403	Reeves, Lucinda J	p	1863	dis		1874	Ukiah, Cal.
404	Reeves, Mary A. (Hotchkin)			d		1870	Ukiah, Cal.
405	Rich, Franklin B	p	1863	dis		1868	Newark Valley.
406	Riley, Loranda Mrs						
407	Rising, Mary (Munson) (Beers)	p	1863	d	June 21,	1874	Liberty.
408	Roberts, Mrs	l	1863	dis		1864	
409	Robinson, Bethiah						
410	Rogers, Alma B. (Truesdell) (Spencer)					1865	Union Center.
411	Rose, L. Josephine (Fritcher)	p	1866	dis			

No.	Name.	Admission.		Removal.	Residence and Remarks.
412	Sairs, Mrs..........	p	1863		
413	Santley, Sarah........	l	1850		
414	Schoonmaker, Maria........	l	1864	d	August, 1873 Valiska, Iowa.
415	Schoonmaker, Sarah J. (West).....	l	1859		
416	Scott, George Henry......	l	1870	dis	1873 Galesburg, Ill.
417	Scott, Jennie R. (Watson)......	l	1870	dis	1873 Galesburg, Ill.
418	Searl, Edward F				
419	Searl, Electa Mrs........				
420	Searles, Addie May.......	p	1874		
421	Severson, Maria A. (Babcock).....	p	1866		
422	Sharpe, Liberty.........	l	1850	r	Tioga.
423	Shaw, Walter S				
424	Shaw, Lucretia (Johnson)......				
425	Shaw, Uriah........	p	1866	d	July 11, 1864
426	Slater, Franklin B	p	1866	dis	1873
427	Slater, Dorus M.........	p	1868		
428	Slater, Phebe Mrs........				
429	Slosson, Sabina (Leonard)......	l	1862	d	January 7, 1867
430	Smith, Starr B.........	l	1850		
431	Smith, Goodrich........	p	1863		
432	Smith, Cornelia Mrs.......	p	1863		
433	Spicer, Phebe A.........	p	1869	d	April, 1873 Tioga.
434	Staples, Elizabeth (Schoonmaker)	p	1862	dis	1864 Illinois.
435	Steele, Adelaide A. (Muzzy)......			sus	
436	Stephenson, Sanford.......			sus	
437	Stevens, Josephine M. (Nye).....	p	1866		
438	Stiles, Charles L........	p	1871		
439	Stiles, Marietta (Archibald)......	p	1863		

No.	Name		Year	Status	Date	Place
440	Strait, Edward E.	p	1872			
441	Stratton, Edward	p	1863			
442	Stroup, Elizabeth (Hutchinson)	p	1863	sns		1867
443	Stuart, Sarah A.					
444	Sykes, Theodore P.					Newark Valley.
445	Sykes, Electa B. (Chapman)	p				Newark Valley.
446	Taft, H. S.	p	1863	dis		1866 Mansville, Mich.
447	Tallmadge, Jane	l		sns		1873 Addison.
448	Taylor, Thomas	l	1864	sns		1873 Westchester.
449	Taylor, Eliza Mrs	l	1864	dis		1869 Brooklyn.
450	Tenney, Jonathan	l	1870	dis		1874 Albany.
451	Tenney, Ellen (LeGro)	l	1870	dis		1874 Albany.
452	Tenney, Hattie Lydia	p	1874	dis		1874 Albany.
453	Terwilliger, Benjamin D					
454	Terwilliger, Rachel Mrs.					
455	Terwilliger, Minnie	p	1873	sns		1873
456	Thatcher, Mary		1868	dis		1868 Cleveland, O.
457	Thomas, Albert R.	p	1863	dis		1868 Cleveland, O.
458	Thomas, Bricea M. (Kilborn)	p	1874			
459	Thomas, Samuel H.	p	1874			
460	Thomas, Delphina A	p	1863	dis		1867
461	Thompson, Frances					
462	Thompson, D. E. Mrs	p				Montague, Mich.
463	Tidd, Minerva	l	1850	ex	March 1, 1855	
464	True, Abner Thrasher	l	1850	d	1863	
465	True, Lydia (Shepardson)	l	1850	dis / d	October 18.1870	1873 Elbridge.
466	True, Albert					
467	True, Anna					
468	Truesdell, Beriah H	l	1850	d	1873	Iowa.
469	Trnesdell, Catharine (Hoagland)	l	1850			Iowa.
470	Truesdell, Phebe (Hoagland)	l		dis		1863 Campville.

No.	Name	Admission		Removal		Residence and Remarks.
471	Truesdell, Aaron Putnam		dis		1863	Cal.
472	Truesdell, Esther E. Mrs.		sns		1873	Libby Prison.
473	Truesdell, Lewis W.		d			
474	Truesdell, Benjauin Franklin					
475	Truesdell, Haunah A.					
476	Truman, Mary Mrs.					
477	Truman, Emily M. (Goodrich)	l 1859	dis		1861	Brooklyn.
478	Tyler, Moses Coit	l 1859	dis		1861	Brooklyn.
479	Tyler, Jennette H. (Gilbert)	l	w			
480	Vinclete, John					
481	Wales, Martha					
482	Walker, Auson					
483	Walker, Betsey C. (Pitcher)					
484	Walker, Edgar A.	p 1868	dis			
485	Walker, Lorin (Auson)	p 1872			1872	
486	Waring, Almerian S.					
487	Warner, Amanda	p 1863	dis			
488	Watrous, Odell J	p 1873	dis			
489	Webster, Lucy Ann					
490	Webster, Elizabeth A. (Johnson)	p 1863	.			
491	West, M. Augusta	f 1873				
492	White, Jane Mrs	l 1873				
493	Whitney, Joseph	l 1862	d	May 10,	1868	
494	Whitney, George	p 1862	d	Feb. 22,	1864	
495	Wiggin, Albert B.		dis		1862	Saugerties.
496	Wiggin, Abigail A. Mrs		d			
497	Wiggin, Ella		dis		1862	
498	Wilcox, Samuel		dis			

No.	Name		Admitted		Dismissed	Date	Residence
499	Wilcox, Eliza Mrs.			d		Feb. 6, 1854	
500	Wilcox, Samuel C.			d		March 26, 1854	
501	Wilcox, Mary (Darling)			dis		1854	Philadelphia, Pa.
502	Williams, Gilbert	1	1850	dis		1855	New Woodstock.
503	Williams, Anna E. (Madan)	1	1850	dis		1855	New Woodstock.
504	Williams, Hiram Greene	1	1850	dis			Susquehanna, Pa.
505	Williams, Sarah J. (Madan)	1	1850	d		1862	Susquehanna, Pa.
506	Williams, Edson	p	1863	dis	May,	1872	Elmira.
507	Williams, Sarah Mrs.	p	1863	dis		1873	Elmira.
508	Williams, Louisa	p	1868			1873	
509	Williams, Lucy Adelaide	p	1868				
510	Williams, Francelia	p	1869	dis			
511	Williams, William	p	1863	sns			Wilkesbarre, Pa.
512	Wilsey, Almira (Angier)	p	1866	sns			
513	Wilson, James	p	1866	dis			
514	Wilson, Caroline Mrs.	p	1854	dis			
515	Witherell, Charles			dis			
516	Witherell, Charles Mrs.			dis			
517	Wood, Seeley	1	1867	dis		1868	Dunkirk.
518	Wood, Susan Mrs.	1	1867	d		1868	Dunkirk.
519	Woodward, Abby A. Mrs.			dis	May 4,	1871	Providence, R. I.
520	Woodworth, Sarah A. (Champlin)	1	1862				Providence, R. I.
521	Wright, Hollister N	1	1862				
522	Wright, Jane C. Mrs.	1	1874				
523	Zimmer, Emma	1					

Summary.

Original members 46
Added by profession..... 190
Added by letter 134
Added by letter or profession...................................... 154

Males 192
Females 332

Whole number... 524
Removed by dismission 168
Removed by death.. 59
Removed by excommunication 8
Removed by withdrawal 9
Removed in mode unknown.................................... 4

Total removed 248

Now on record 276
Suspended 38

In good standing.. 238

Notes.

I. Aug. 7, 1810.—At the first organization of the "Congregational Society of Owego," Solomon Jones, Caleb Leach, Abraham Hoagland, William Camp, James Pumpelly, and Eleazer Dana were elected trustees.

II. July 24, 1817.—At the formation of the first Congregational Church in connection with the above Congregational Society, it was constituted of the following eleven members : Nathan Camp, Solomon Jones, William Jones, Lorenzo Reeves, Clarissa Jones, Margery Jones, Ruth Goodrich, Sarah Goodrich, Sally Penfield, Mary Perry, and Dolly Talcott,—all now deceased.

III. Over this church there have been the following pastors: Hezekiah May, July, 1817, to Spring of 1818; Horatio I. Lombard, Oct. 28, 1818, to Aug. 2, 1827; Aaron Putnam, Dec. 6, 1827, to Dec. 28, 1831; Charles White, April 19, 1832, to May 25, 1841; Samuel C. Wilcox, May 24, 1842, to April 30, 1846; Seth Williston, July, 1846, to April 4, 1847; Philip C. Hay, April 15, 1847, to Oct. 7, 1855; S. H. Cox, October, 1855, to December, 1856; S. H. Hall, Feb. 24, 1857, to June 1, 1864; Solon Cobb, Nov. 8, 1865, to September, 1869; S. T. Clarke, February, 1870,—most of whom were Congregationalists.

IV. July 31, 1831.—This same church, under the pastorate of Aaron Putnam, so far adopted the Presbyterian mode of conducting church affairs as to elect Solomon Jones, William Platt, Eleazer Dana, and

William Pumpelly, Elders, without changing the name of the church, or giving the entire management of its affairs into the sessions.

V. Dec. 31, 1849.—From the well kept records of the old Congregational church, now called the *Presbyterian* church of Owego, is gathered the list of persons who, in due form, asked dismission from the said church to form the present Congregational church, and were regularly dismissed, on this day, for this purpose. (See page 21.)

VI. Aug. 1, 1850.—The "*Independent* Congregational Society," in connection with the above new church, being duly organized at the Court House, the following persons were elected the first Trustees: Newell Matson, Abner T. True, James W. Lamoureux, Erastus Meacham, Henry W. Camp, and Gilbert Williams.

VII. Feb. 3, 1852, the house was formally dedicated to the service of the Lord.

VIII. Feb. 4, 1852.—The pews were first rented and assessed 12 per cent on value, for support of the Society.

IX. The old bell, weighing 1800 lbs., was hung in the tower, 134 feet high. It was taken down and replaced by a new one, September, 1874.

X. May 14, 1854.—The Society was out of debt—the balance of about $4,000, in the church building, having been assumed and paid by Newell Matson, now of Chicago.

XI. The Committee who bought the organ, altered and repaired the main edifice, and made the addition of conference room and parlor in 1863, consisted of David Goodrich, John J. Hooker S. S. Allen, D. H. Bloodgood, and M. F. Howes.

XII. The "Weekly Contribution Plan" of church support was adopted April 1, 1872, and has given great satisfaction.

XIII. The most marked revival seasons appear to have been during the ministries of Wilcox, Corning, Bartlett, Everest, and Bulkley—all but the first, settled pastors.

XIV. The General Association of New York held its annual sessions with this church in 1853 and 1866.

XV. The Susquehanna Conference of Churches met with this church 1st Tuesday in June, 1852, and June 7, 1863; the Susquehanna Association, Feb. 7, 1871, and Feb. 3, 1874.

XVI. In 1854, it was voted by the church that the privilege of speaking and praying in church meetings should be allowed to females.

XVII. The Manual of 1857 contained a list of 141 members, — male, —— female. Of these 33 were among the original members.

The Manual of 1867 contained a list of 226 members—76 male, 150 female. Of these, 12 were among the original members.

XVIII. UNION SOLDIERS.—Timothy Clark, Capt. 106th Pa. Vols.; Lewis W. Truesdell, Capt. 21st N. Y. Cavalry; Benjamin F. Truesdell, private 21st N. Y. Cavalry; George Forsyth, Co. I, 50th N. Y. Vols.; Arthur C. Danforth, John J. Curtis, William C. Foster, Edward P. Jones, John Deming, Franklin B. Rich—10.

XIX. LAWYERS.—None.

XX. PHYSICIANS.—John Frank, Aaron P. Truesdell, Geo. H. Scott, Charles L. Stiles, James Wilson, William H. Cole—6.

XXI. TEACHERS.—Albert B. Wiggin, James M. Burt, William H. Cole, Jonathan Tenney—4.

XXII. MINISTERS OE THE GOSPEL.—Samuel C. Wilcox, Beriah H. Truesdell, Corbin Kidder, William H. Corning, Washington Gladden, Lewis E. Matson, Albert True, William A. Bartlett, Henry M. Higley, Frederick A. Parmenter, Moses C. Tyler, George Whitney, Chas. H. A. Bulkley, Charles H. Crawford, Jonathan Tenney, Dwight W. Marsh—16.

XXIII. CHURCH OFFICERS.—*Deacons.*—Newell Matson, 1850 62; John Perry, 1850; James W. Lamoureux, 1850-59; Abner Turasher True, 1850-63; Albert B. Wiggin, 1859-62; Timothy Clark, 1859-62; Sylvester S Allen, 1862-69; Thomas Evans, Jr., 1862-71; John J. Hooker, 1862; Theodore P. Sykes, 1871-73; James Monroe Hastings, 1871; John B. G. Babcock, 1874.

Clerks—Henry W. Camp, 1850-1854; John Danforth, 1854-1857; Abner T True, 1857-1863; William D. Cady, 1863-1871; James M. Hastings, 1871-1874; Dwight W. Marsh, 1874.

XXIV. SABBATH SCHOOL SUPERINTENDENTS.—John Danforth, Timothy Clark, Sylvester S. Allen, John J. Hooker, Charles H. Everest, William H. Cole, James C. Beecher, Jonathan Tenney, James M. Hastings.

XXV. CHORISTERS.—Erastus Meacham, N. J. Loomis, —— Swift, Elihu Hosford, Watson L. Hoskins, William D. Cady, Norton A. Stevens, Fayette F. Hoskins.

XXVI. ORGANISTS.—Prof. Joseph Raff, Mrs. W. D. Cady, Mrs. J. Tenney, Mrs. N. A. Stevens, Mrs. D. W. Marsh.

XXVII. SOCIETY OFFICERS.—*Trustees.*—Newell Matson, 1850-1860; Abner T. True, 1850-1860; James W. Lamoureux, 1850-1859; Erastus Meacham, 1850-1855; Henry W. Camp, 1850-1856 and 1858-1859; Gilbert Williams, 1850-1853; John Danforth, 1853-1858; David Goodrich, 1855-1866; John R. Chatfield, 1856-1859; Frank L. Jones, 1859-1862 and 1866-1869; William D. Ireland, 1859-1861; Thomas Evans,

Jr., 1859-1871 ; Sylvester S. Allen, 1861-1869 ; John J. Hooker, 1861-1865 and 1866 ; James M. Burt, 1862-1863 ; Darwin H. Bloodgood, 1862-1866 ; John B. G. Babcock, 1863-1869 ; Ethelbert Ogden, 1865-1867 ; James Wilson, 1867-1870 ; Henry Campb ll, 1869 ; Cyrus W. Gray, 1869-1871 ; Theodore P. Sykes, 1869-1873 ; James M. Hastings, 1869 ; George H. Scott, 1870-1872 ; Lee N. Chamberlain, 1871 ; Miles F. Howes, 1871 ; Benjamin W. Brown, 1872 ; Jerry M. Hollensworth, 1873.

Treasurers—Henry W Camp, 1850-1856 and 1858-1859 ; John Danforth, 1856-1858 ; Thomas Evans, 1859-1867 ; Frank L. Jones, 1867-1869 ; Cyrus W. Gray, 1869-1871 ; James M. Hastings, 1871.

XXVIII. CALENDAR.—*Sunday Services.*—Preaching, 10½ o'clock A. M. and 7½ o'clock P. M. Sabbath School, 12 M. Weekly Household Meeting, Tuesday evening. Church Conference and Prayer Meeting, Thursday evening. Ladies' Benevolent Society, Thursday afternoon. Preparatory Lecture, Thursday evening before Communion. Lord's Supper, first Sabbaths in February, April, June, August, October, and November. Weekly collection for Society expenses, every Sunday morning. Benevolent collections for Am. Board of Home Missions, Am. Miss. Asso., and the Bible Soc., once each quarter. Financial year, April 1. Pew renting, April 1. Society annual meeting, first Tuesday in August. Church annual meeting, last Wednesday in December. Quarterly pay days, 1st February, 1st May, 1st August, 1st November. Pastor's vacation, July or August, 4 weeks.